The Gurgle Gloop

Poems by Charles Thomson

Contents

The Gurgle Gloop	2
Something In My Soup	4
The Lolly	6
What Did Daddy Say?	8
In Hospital	10
Stronger Than You	12
Get The Ball	14
Bored Today	16
First Day At School	18
Edmund's Curled Up	20
Janet Bawled Her Head Off	22
Index Of First Lines	24

The Glurgle Gloooooooooooop

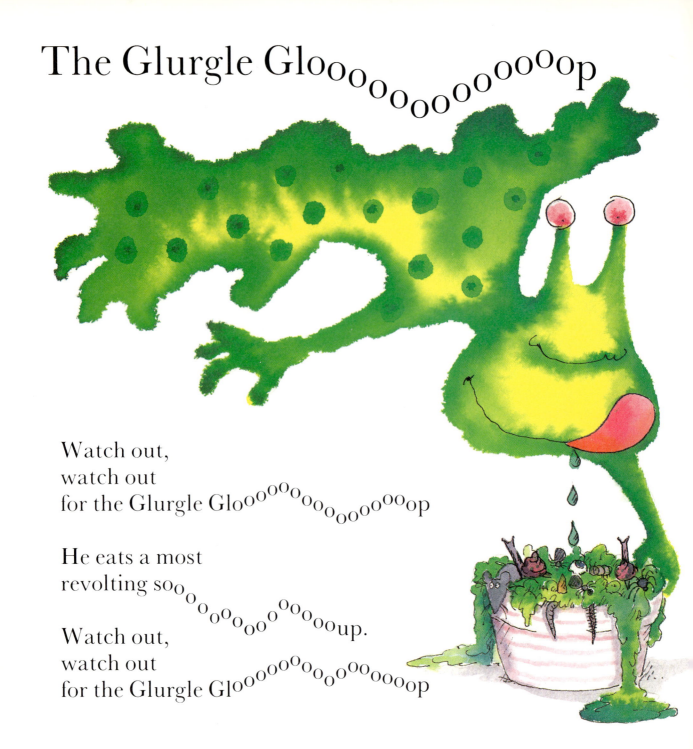

Watch out,
watch out
for the Glurgle Glooooooooooooooop

He eats a most
revolting sooooooooooooooooup.

Watch out,
watch out
for the Glurgle Gloooooooooooooop

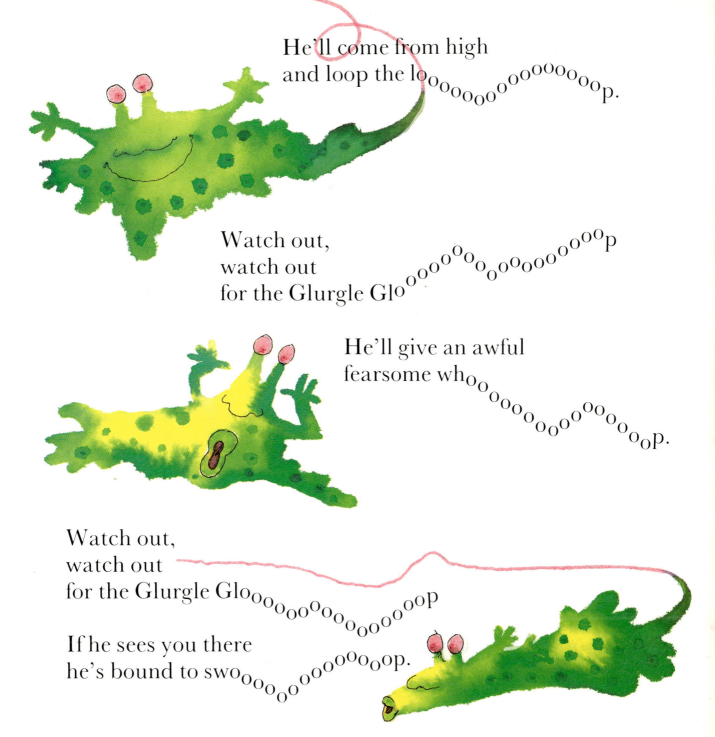

He'll come from high
and loop the loooooooooooooooop.

Watch out,
watch out
for the Glurgle Gloooooooooooooooooop

He'll give an awful
fearsome whoooooooooooooooop.

Watch out,
watch out
for the Glurgle Glooooooooooooooop

If he sees you there
he's bound to swoooooooooooooop.

Something In My Soup

'What's that in my soup, mummy?'
'Oh no, it's the baby's dummy!'

The Lolly

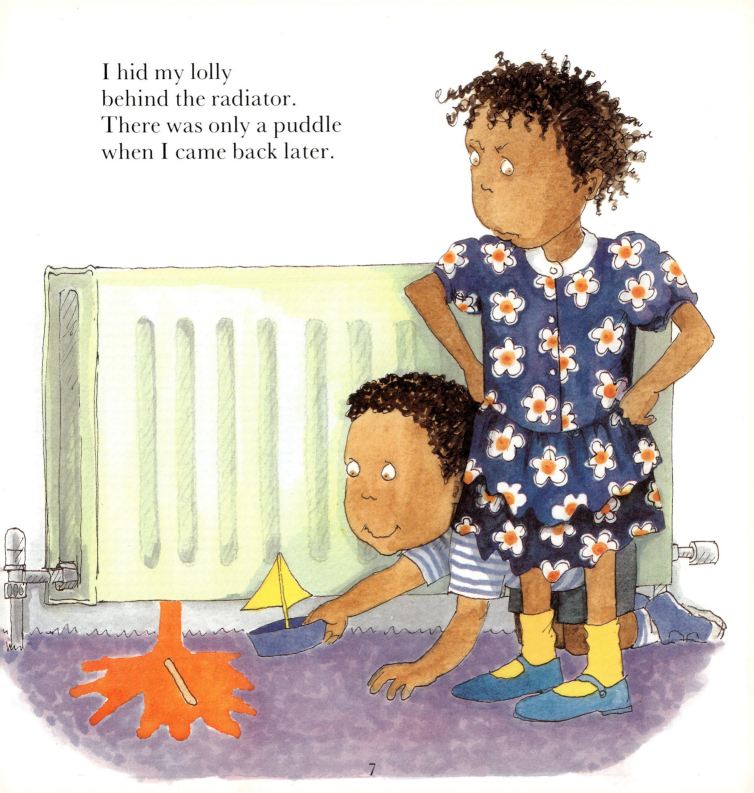

What Did Daddy Say?

Daddy drove the car
into the wall today.
I'm afraid I can't tell you
what I heard him say.

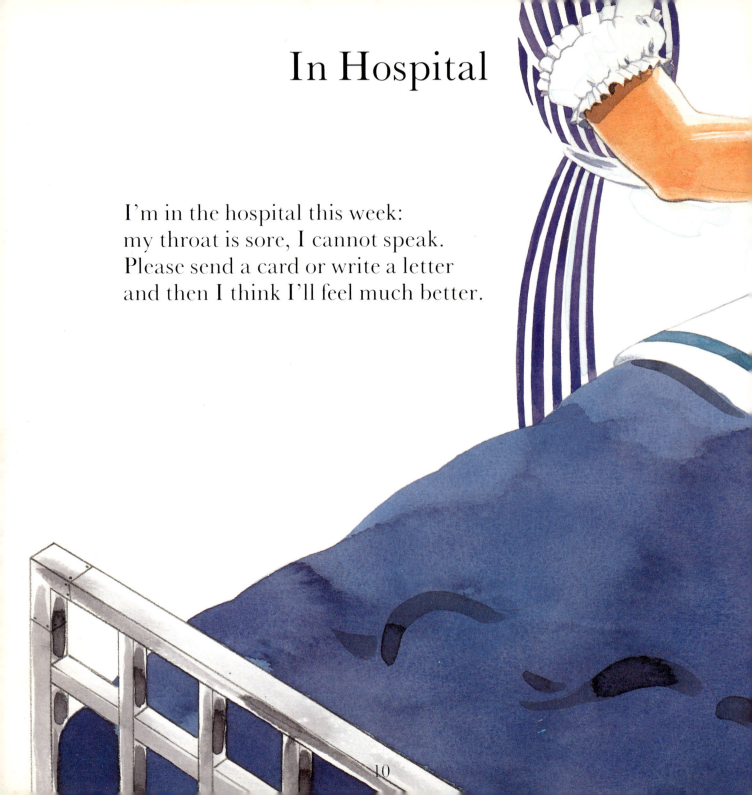

In Hospital

I'm in the hospital this week:
my throat is sore, I cannot speak.
Please send a card or write a letter
and then I think I'll feel much better.

Stronger Than You

I'm stronger than you,
that's easy to see.
It's just that you're three times
the size of me.

Get The Ball

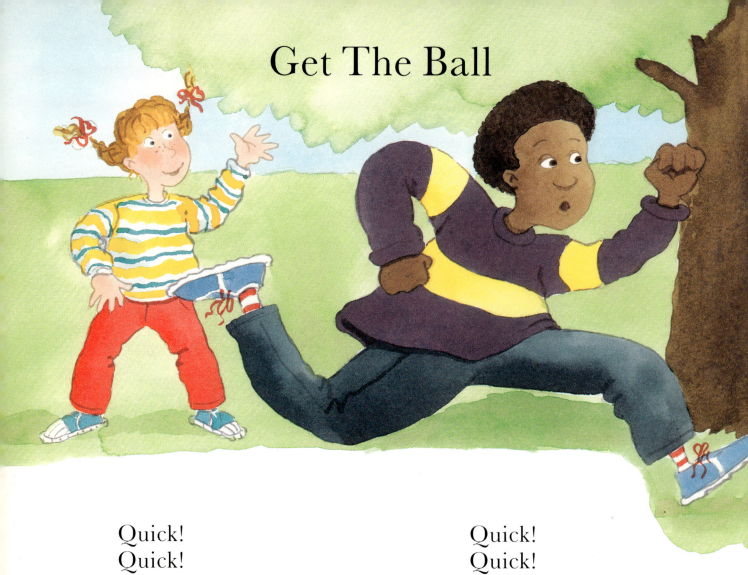

Quick!
Quick!
Kick!
Kick!

Get the ball.
Don't fall.

Quick!
Quick!
Kick!
Kick!

By the tree.
To me! To me!

Oh dear!

Muddy behind.
Never mind.

Bored Today

I'm bored today –
I've got nothing to do.
I get like that sometimes.
Do you?

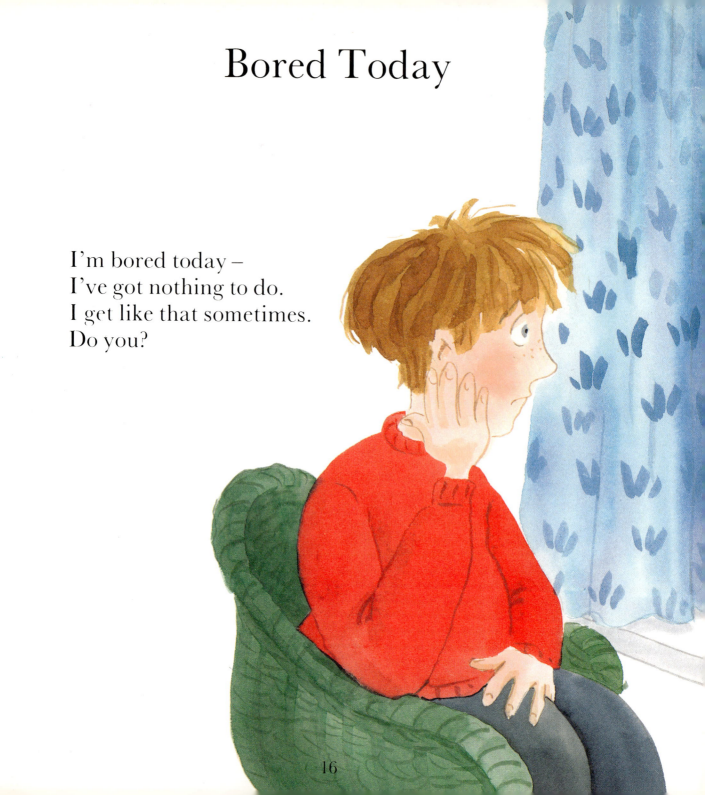

First Day At School

My new friend and I
feel a bit scared,
but things are easier
when they're shared.

Edmund's Curled Up

Edmund's curled up
in the chair
and on his face
is a solemn stare.
He wants us all
to go away.
What's wrong with him?
He will not say.

Janet Bawled Her Head Off

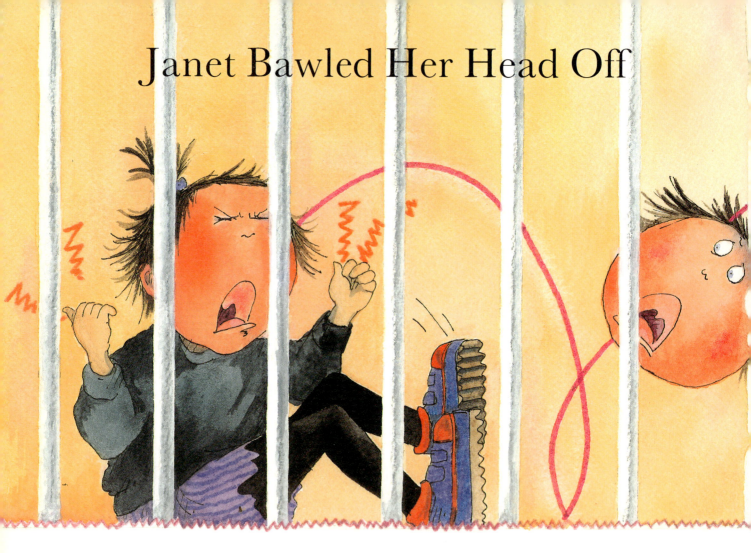

Janet bawled her head off:
it fell upon the floor,
went bouncing down the stairs
and vanished out the door.

Index Of First Lines

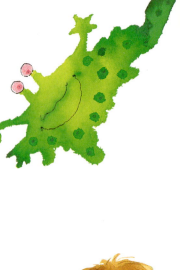

Daddy drove the car	8
Edmund's curled up	20
I hid my lolly	6
I'm bored today	16
I'm in the hospital this week	10
I'm stronger than you	12
Janet bawled her head off	22
My new friend and I	18
Quick!	14
Watch out	2
'What's that in my soup, mummy?'	4